# CLASSICS FOR KIDS:
## FOUR PLAYS ADAPTED FROM THE BOOKS OF DON FREEMAN

by Wysteria Edwards

www.youthplays.com
info@youthplays.com
424-703-5315

*Classics for Kids: Four Plays Adapted from the Books of Don Freeman (A Pocket for Corduroy; Dandelion; Manuelo, the Playing Mantis; Mop Top)* © 2011 Wysteria Edwards
All rights reserved. ISBN 978-1-62088-218-4.

**Caution:** This play is fully protected under the copyright laws of the United States of America, Canada, the British Commonwealth and all other countries of the copyright union and is subject to royalty for all performances including but not limited to professional, amateur, charity and classroom whether admission is charged or presented free of charge.

**Reservation of Rights:** This play is the property of the author and all rights for its use are strictly reserved and must be licensed by his representative, YouthPLAYS. This prohibition of unauthorized professional and amateur stage presentations extends also to motion pictures, recitation, lecturing, public reading, radio broadcasting, television, video and the rights of adaptation or translation into non-English languages.

**Performance Licensing and Royalty Payments:** Amateur and stock performance rights are administered exclusively by YouthPLAYS. No amateur, stock or educational theatre groups or individuals may perform this play without securing authorization and royalty arrangements in advance from YouthPLAYS. Required royalty fees for performing this play are available online at www.YouthPLAYS.com. Royalty fees are subject to change without notice. Required royalties must be paid each time this play is performed and may not be transferred to any other performance entity. All licensing requests and inquiries should be addressed to YouthPLAYS.

**Author Credit:** All groups or individuals receiving permission to produce this play must give the author(s) credit in any and all advertisements and publicity relating to the production of this play. The author's billing must appear directly below the title on a separate line with no other accompanying written matter. The name of the author(s) must be at least 50% as large as the title of the play. No person or entity may receive larger or more prominent credit than that which is given to the author(s) and the name of the author(s) may not be abbreviated or otherwise altered from the form in which it appears in this Play.

**Publisher Attribution:** All programs, advertisements, flyers or other printed material must include the following notice:
*Produced by special arrangement with YouthPLAYS (www.youthplays.com).*

**Prohibition of Unauthorized Copying:** Any unauthorized copying of this book or excerpts from this book, whether by photocopying, scanning, video recording or any other means, is strictly prohibited by law. This book may only be copied by licensed productions with the purchase of a photocopy license, or with explicit permission from YouthPLAYS.

**Trade Marks, Public Figures & Musical Works:** This play may contain references to brand names or public figures. All references are intended only as parody or other legal means of expression. This play may also contain suggestions for the performance of a musical work (either in part or in whole). YouthPLAYS has not obtained performing rights of these works unless explicitly noted. The direction of such works is only a playwright's suggestion, and the play producer should obtain such permissions on their own. The website for the U.S. copyright office is *http://www.copyright.gov*.

## COPYRIGHT RULES TO REMEMBER

1. To produce this play, you must receive prior written permission from YouthPLAYS and pay the required royalty.

2. You must pay a royalty each time the play is performed in the presence of audience members outside of the cast and crew. Royalties are due whether or not admission is charged, whether or not the play is presented for profit, for charity or for educational purposes, or whether or not anyone associated with the production is being paid.

3. No changes, including cuts or additions, are permitted to the script without written prior permission from YouthPLAYS.

4. Do not copy this book or any part of it without written permission from YouthPLAYS.

5. Credit to the author and YouthPLAYS is required on all programs and other promotional items associated with this play's performance.

When you pay royalties, you are recognizing the hard work that went into creating the play and making a statement that a play is something of value. We think this is important, and we hope that everyone will do the right thing, thus allowing playwrights to generate income and continue to create wonderful new works for the stage.

> Plays are owned by the playwrights who wrote them. Violating a playwright's copyright is a very serious matter and violates both United States and international copyright law. Infringement is punishable by actual damages and attorneys' fees, statutory damages of up to $150,000 per incident, and even possible criminal sanctions. **Infringement is theft. Don't do it.**

Have a question about copyright? Please contact us by email at info@youthplays.com or by phone at 424-703-5315. When in doubt, please ask.

## TABLE OF CONTENTS

| | |
|---|---|
| *A Pocket for Corduroy* | 5 |
| *Dandelion* | 12 |
| *Manuelo, the Playing Mantis* | 18 |
| *Mop Top* | 23 |

# A POCKET FOR CORDUROY

A ten-minute play adapted from the book by Don Freeman

CAST OF CHARACTERS

LISA, a young girl.
MOTHER
CORDUROY, male, a young stuffed bear.
ARTIST, a young man or woman.
MANAGER, male or female.

*(Lights up on a stage with bright colored buildings and storefronts: Pandro's Laundromat. There are people busy loading their wash into larger-than-life washers and dryers. Everything in the laundromat should be magnified as a small stuffed bear would see it. LISA, a young girl, and her MOTHER enter. Mother is carrying bags of laundry, and Lisa is walking with her stuffed bear, CORDUROY. He is scruffy brown, much like the color of an acorn and wears a pair of bright emerald-green, corduroy overalls. He is Lisa's best friend and very curious. MUSIC plays as they enter the scene. Corduroy is full of life and eager to tell his story. He walks forward to address the audience.)*

**CORDUROY:** Why, hello! *(He waits for a response:)* My name is Corduroy. As you can see, I'm a stuffed bear. And that is my special friend, Lisa, and her mother. Do you have any special friends? Lisa has loved me for as long as I can remember, which isn't such a long time for a bear who has stuffing inside his head for brains. I used to live in a toy store! A large, bright, wonderful place where I got to watch people all day long. Then one day, Lisa came and took me home with her. I have a cozy bed and lots of love. We even get to go for adventures in the park, at her school...oh, and one time we went to the circus! Today I'm excited because we are going to a special place where they wash clothes...it's called a... *(He can't remember:)* Uh, oh. I seem to have forgotten the name of it. Do you know what it is? *(Waits for the children to answer:)* Yes, yes...I remember now. It's called a LAUNDROMAT. *(He giggles:)* What a fun word! *(He tries it again in a silly, sing-song voice:)* LAUNDROMAT!! *(Beat.)* Sometimes when people do not own a washer and dryer they do their washing in a place like this. Come and explore with me!

*(The laundromat is a busy place. There are people folding clothes, replacing loads in the machines, reading magazines, etc. Lisa moves Corduroy to a large chair, much too big for him.)*

**LISA:** Now, Corduroy, you sit right here and wait for me. I'm going to help with our wash.

*(He tries to wait by swinging his feet around. He overhears Lisa's mother:)*

**MOTHER:** Be sure to take everything out of your pockets, Lisa dear. You don't want your precious things to get all wet and soapy.

*(Corduroy is confused...perplexed. Looking down at his overalls, he frowns.)*

**CORDUROY:** *(To the audience:)* Pockets? What's a pocket? I don't have a pocket!

*(Slowly he slides off the chair.)*

I must find something to make a pocket out of.

*(He begins to look around. There is a pile of fancy towels and washcloths. He takes the time to play with them. Placing one around his head like a turban, we hear SNAKE-CHARMER MUSIC. A red towel transforms him into a bullfighter.)*

None of these seem to be the right size or color for a pocket.

*(He sees a huge stack of colorful clothes in a laundry bag.)*

Oh, wow, look! There ought to be something in there to make a pocket out of.

*(Without hesitation, he quickly crawls inside the bag full of wet pieces of laundry. He pokes his head out and speaks to the audience:)*

This must be a cave. I've always wanted to live in a dark, cool cave. Do you think I'll find a pocket in here? Let's look and see.

*(He disappears into the bag as Lisa turns around to discover him gone. Her Mother has finished their laundry.)*

**LISA:** Oh, Mommy! Corduroy isn't here where I left him!

**MOTHER:** I'm sorry, honey, but the laundromat will be closing soon and we must be getting home.

**LISA:** But Mommy, I can't leave without Corduroy! He'll be frightened.

**MOTHER:** You can come back tomorrow. I'm sure you will find him. Come along.

*(Lisa and Mother exit. A YOUNG MAN [or WOMAN] wearing an artist's beret begins to take the wet laundry out of Corduroy's "cave" when the bear tumbles out onto the floor.)*

**ARTIST:** How in thunder did you get mixed up with my things?

**CORDUROY:** The cave was damp and now I have the sh...shhh...shivers.

**ARTIST:** Well, the least I can do for you is give your overalls a good drying.

*(He unbuttons Corduroy's shoulder straps and puts his overalls in the dryer. The clothes dryer. The clothes begin to swirl around inside. The artist becomes inspired and takes out his sketch pad.)*

**CORDUROY:** I could get dizzy watching those clothes go around and around, couldn't you?

**ARTIST:** *(Excited:)* This would make a wonderful painting! I can hardly wait to get back to my studio.

*(There is a loud BUZZ signaling that the clothes are dry. The artist takes out the overalls and helps Corduroy dress again.)*

Ah, there you go. Nice, dry overalls for a cute stuffed bear. You sit here right beside these soap flakes and wait for your little friend to come back and find you.

*(He sits Corduroy by a big box of soap flakes. The Artist looks back at Corduroy.)*

I wonder who that bear belongs to. He should have his name someplace. He's too fine a fellow to be lost.

*(The MANAGER, who has been sweeping, calls out to the customers as the Artist exits.)*

**MANAGER:** Closing time! Everybody out!

*(The Manager turns out the lights. As soon as they go out, Corduroy begins his search again.)*

**CORDUROY:** I still need to find my pocket.

*(He looks in the soap flakes box.)*

*(Indicating the soap flakes:)* Do you think I will find a pocket in here? We might be surprised. I should check it out.

*(The soap flakes fall all over covering him.)*

Is this snow? I've always wanted to play in the snow!

*(He throws it up in the air making a "snow bear.")*

*(Stopping suddenly:)* Oh! I still need to find that pocket!

*(He begins to slip and slide on the soap flakes.)*

Look at me! I'm ice skating! I've always wanted to ice skate!

*(He falls right into a wheeling laundry basket. His mood instantly becomes sad.)*

This must be a cage. I've never wanted to live inside a cage like a bear in the zoo.

*(He is getting sleepy.)*

Finding a pocket is very tiring work. Wouldn't you agree? Perhaps I should just rest awhile to replenish my energy.

*(He nods off to sleep. Time passes and the sun gradually comes up again. We see the world come back to life, as the Manager enters and begins to clean up the soap flakes. Lisa comes running in and the bell on the door JINGLES.)*

**MANAGER:** Good morning.

**LISA:** Hello. I left something here yesterday. May I look around?

**MANAGER:** Certainly, my customers are always leaving things. Let me help you.

*(They begin their search for Corduroy. Lisa searches under chairs and in back of the washing machines. The Manager finally sees Corduroy still asleep in the basket.)*

Is this what you are looking for?

**LISA:** Yes, yes! He's my best friend! *(Beat.)* So this is where you've been, you little rascal! It's time I took you home! *(To the Manager:)* Thank you!

*(Lisa and Corduroy exit the laundromat and walk home. They enter her bedroom, where there is a little bed for Corduroy next to hers.)*

I thought I told you to wait for me. Why did you wander away?

**CORDUROY:** I went looking for a pocket.

**LISA:** Oh, Corduroy! Why didn't you tell me you wanted a pocket?

*(She takes out a purple pocket and "sews" it on. He admires it proudly.)*

**CORDUROY:** *(To the audience:)* Look, friends! I have a pocket. My very own pocket! Do you have any pockets you'd like to show me? *(Responds to what children show him:)* Wow! Look at all those wonderful pockets. I feel so special.

**LISA:** *(Tucking a card into his pocket:)* And here is a card I've made with your name on it for you to keep tucked inside.

**CORDUROY:** I've always wanted a purple pocket with my name tucked inside.

**LISA:** *(Laughing at him:)* Oh, Corduroy...

*(And they nuzzle noses...the best of friends. Blackout.)*

# DANDELION

A ten-minute play adapted from the book by Don Freeman

CAST OF CHARACTERS

DANDELION, a lion.
LOU KANGAROO
RABBIT
THEODORE THE TAILOR
HAPPY CRANE
JENNIFER GIRAFFE

*(The sun is coming up on a small bedroom. We HEAR the song "Somewhere Over the Rainbow/What a Wonderful World" by Israel Kamakawiwo'ole. There is a brass bed, small dresser, a stool with an alarm clock, and a framed picture of a lion wearing a crown with the word "FATHER" underneath it. DANDELION, a lion, wakes up. He stretches, yawns and jumps out of bed. He is dressed in white pajamas with orange stripes. Excitedly, he does his daily exercises.)*

**DANDELION:** I wonder if the mail has come?

*(He puts on his sweater and hurries outside to the mailbox. There is a letter, written in fancy, gold ink. The initials J.G. are written on the back. Reading the letter to the audience:)*

"Dear Dandelion, You are invited to my tea-and-taffy party on Saturday afternoon at half-past three. Come as you are. Sincerely, Jennifer Giraffe." *(Beat.)* Why, that's today! It's a good thing I planned to get a haircut!

*(He comically and quickly eats his breakfast, and washes/wipes the dishes.)*

*(Counting the wipes on the dishes:)* 1, 2, 3.

*(Placing the dish in the drying rack. He makes his bed nice and neat, and runs off to the barbershop to see LOU KANGAROO. A barber chair is waiting for him. First, Lou trims Dandelion's hair with exceptionally large scissors. Next he "shampoos," placing a large bubble cap on him. RABBIT sits down on a stool to give him a manicure.)*

**LOU KANGAROO:** So, what's the occasion?

**DANDELION:** Jennifer Giraffe is having a tea-and-taffy party today at half past three.

**RABBIT:** We're invited too! I just love tea-and-taffy parties, don't you?

**LOU KANGAROO:** We'll have to give you a new hair-do for the occasion!

**RABBIT:** Oh, yes. Maybe a wave would help.

*(Lou holds up a magazine that shows a picture of a distinguished lion with a curled mane.)*

**LOU KANGAROO:** It's what all the well-dressed lions are wearing this year!

**DANDELION:** Then it's exactly what I need!

**LOU KANGAROO:** Let's get that mane curled.

*(The song "Steppin' Out With My Baby" by Fred Astaire begins to play. The lights transition...there is a drum-roll. In the dark, an extremely curly wig is placed on Dandelion. Lights up. Lou Kangaroo spins the chair around to face the audience.)*

Ta da!

**DANDELION:** I look magnificent.

**RABBIT:** Now you need a new outfit!

**DANDELION:** I really should wear something more elegant than a sweater to the party.

*(He makes his way to the tailor shop. There is a black and white checkered jacket next to a sign that reads, "READY TO WEAR." THEODORE THE TAILOR greets him. He is a bear. Taking the jacket off the form, he helps Dandelion put it on.)*

**THEODORE THE TAILOR:** This jacket is the very newest style, and it just fits you. All you need now is a cap and a cane. Happy Crane will be glad to help you.

**DANDELION:** *(Admiring himself to the audience:)* What a dapper dandy I've become!

*(HAPPY CRANE has a sign on an easel that says, "LET HAPPY MAKE YOU LOOK SNAPPY." He hands Dandelion a cane and places a top hat on his head.)*

*(To Crane:)* Dapper?

**HAPPY CRANE:** Dandy. For sure.

*(Dandelion looks at his watch.)*

**DANDELION:** It's nearly half past three! I've just time to get something for my hostess. A bouquet of dandelions would be perfect.

*(He is handed a bouquet by Happy Crane from a vase in the shop.)*

**HAPPY CRANE:** Here, take these!

*(A tall door emerges with several steps in front of it.)*

**DANDELION:** *(To the audience:)* I bet you are thinking, "That is quite a gigantic door!" But have you ever lived with a giraffe? They take up a great deal of space! I better knock before it's too late.

*(He knocks on the door and it opens to reveal an 18-foot giraffe puppet, JENNIFER GIRAFFE. There is a long string of pearls around her neck, and she is wearing lipstick. Her long eyelashes are curled, and there is a bow in her hair.)*

**JENNIFER GIRAFFE:** Yes? What can I do for you?

**DANDELION:** *(Confused:)* Why, I've come for your tea-and-taffy party.

**JENNIFER GIRAFFE:** Oh, I'm sorry, sir, but you are not anyone I know. You must have come to the wrong address.

*(She closed the door on Dandelion's face. He knocks again and again.)*

**DANDELION:** I'm Dandelion! You've made a mighty mistake!

*(He lets out a loud roar and then sits down on the steps.)*

*(To the audience:)* Why doesn't she recognize me? Aren't I still Dandelion? I have to think of what to do.

*(He begins pacing back and forth. The sky grows dark. He looks up into the sky. We hear thunder boom and see lightning crash.)*

*(To the audience:)* It looks like it's going to rain.

*(His bouquet is carried off by the wind. It begins to rain metallic glitter down on him. The stage goes crazy with a storm. Meanwhile he removes the curly wig and transfers back to his generic one. He runs under the shelter of a willow tree. When the sun comes out again, he emerges.)*

*(To the audience:)* I better take off this jacket. I'm much too warm now. Luckily, I kept on my sweater!

*(He slowly makes his way to sit on Jennifer Giraffe's steps again. Three dandelions poke out underneath the front stairs.)*

*(To the audience:)* Oh, look! Three dandelions. They must have been protected from the wind and the rain. *(Beat.)* I think I'll pick them and try again.

*(He picks the flowers for his friend and knocks on the door. Jennifer Giraffe emerges.)*

**JENNIFER GIRAFFE:** Well, well! If it isn't our friend Dandelion at last! We've been waiting for you for the past hour. I do hope you weren't caught in that awful cloudburst!

*(Inside are Lou Kangaroo, Rabbit, Happy Crane and Theodore the Tailor. They greet him heartily.)*

Oh, Dandelion, you should have seen the silly-looking lion who came to the door earlier.

*(Dandelion almost spills his tea as he begins to laugh.)*

**DANDELION:** That was me! I was that silly-looking lion!

**JENNIFER GIRAFFE:** Oh my! I do apologize for having closed the door on you. I promise never to do such a thing again. I just didn't recognize you.

**DANDELION:** And I promise you I will never again try to turn myself into a stylish dandy. *(Sipping his tea:)* From now on I'll always be just plain me!

*(Blackout. End of play.)*

# MANUELO, THE PLAYING MANTIS

A ten-minute play adapted from the book by Don Freeman

### CAST OF CHARACTERS

MANUELO, a praying mantis who loves music and wants to make an instrument.

CRICKET

FROG

ELK

KATYDID

SPIDER, a friend who helps Manuel build a cello to make music.

### SETTING

A meadow.

*(CLASSICAL MUSIC playing in a park concert. MANUELO, the praying mantis, listens to the music.)*

**MANUELO:** Ah, I love the sound of a symphony, don't you? Listen! I hear trumpets, a flute, the harp and a cello. The instruments work together to create the most beautiful sounds. I wish I could be a musician. Perhaps I can make my own music. I've seen a cricket rub his legs together and the sounds were lovely.

*(Rubbing his legs together, but no sound. CRICKET appears from behind a tree.)*

**CRICKET:** Clickety-clack! A mantis can't make music the way I can. Listen to me!

*(She makes her CRICKET SOUNDS.)*

You are just a mantis, a silly, silly mantis.

*(She disappears behind a tree.)*

**MANUELO:** There must be something I can do! I know, I'll make a flute!

*(He finds a hollow cattail, and nibbles several tiny holes along the stem.)*

Just look at my marvelous flute! Surely, it will make beautiful music!

*(He blows on the flute but it makes no sound. FROG appears from behind a tree.)*

**FROG:** Gerumph! Gerumph! We frogs know how to croak. Now *that* is music! A mantis can't make music the way frogs can.

*(He makes his FROG SOUNDS.)*

You're just a mantis, a silly, silly mantis.

*(Frog hops away behind the tree.)*

**MANUELO:** I just know that I can be a musician!

*(He spies a trumpet vine clinging to the wall.)*

Ah ha! Just the thing I need! I'll make a horn to play!

*(He snips a flower off of the vine and holds it up like a trumpet. An ELK enters.)*

**ELK:** Her-hoon! Her-hoon! You can't make a sound like I can. You're just a mantis, a silly, silly mantis.

**MANUELO:** My trumpet will make the most marvelous of sounds! Listen!

*(He blows and blows, but no sound comes out. The Elk laughs and exits behind the tree.)*

I refuse to give up!

*(He scans around and spies a vine on the ground.)*

At last, just what I want!

*(Bending down, he twists the vine into a harp shape. He takes cobwebs and fixes the strings onto it, trying to make a harp.)*

The sounds of a harp make you feel like you're floating in the breeze. Wait until you hear it!

*(Stroking the "strings" with his fingers, the cobwebs break.)*

Oh, no! The harp isn't the instrument for me. Alas, I am feeling very sad, very sad indeed.

*(A KATYDID emerges from behind the tree.)*

**KATYDID:** Katydid, katydid! Don't you know a mantis can't make music the way we can? You're just a mantis, a silly, silly mantis.

*(A SPIDER from up above calls down to them.)*

**SPIDER:** Take heart, my good fellow. I know how you feel. I can't make music either. *(To the Katydid:)* Shoo, you!

*(The Katydid exits behind the tree.)*

I've been watching you all evening. If you do as I tell you, maybe together we can make a cello.

**MANUELO:** I'd forgotten about the cello! That is such a beautiful instrument.

**SPIDER:** I would love to help you, but you must promise me one thing.

**MANUELO:** What is that?

**SPIDER:** You must not eat me.

**MANUELO:** Oh, no...of course not. You are my friend.

**SPIDER:** Very well. First you must fetch me an empty walnut shell and a stick with a curlicue on the end.

*(Manuelo finds an empty walnut and a stick with a curlicue on the end. He rushes back to the spider.)*

**MANUELO:** Will these work?

**SPIDER:** Wonderful! Now, fix the stick tightly to the shell and I will spin strings for you.

*(She quickly spins four, strong silken threads which he attaches to the cello over the curlicue stick.)*

All we need now is a bow. Can you think of something that will do the trick?

**MANUELO:** Yes, yes! I know! I saw a bluebird's feather that should make a splendid bow!

*(He retrieves the bow from behind a rock.)*

**SPIDER:** Now the only thing left to do is to play. Try it!

*(Manuelo begins to bow and the most beautiful MELODY fills the air. The Spider dances to the music. Gradually, the other animals come out to investigate. They form a semi-circle around Manuelo, and join in making their own unique music. Creating a symphony.)*

**MANUELO:** Why, I've created my own symphony!

*(Slowly, they leave one by one, until Manuelo is left alone on stage.)*

Now that, my friends, was music.

*(Blackout.)*

# MOP TOP

A ten-minute play adapted from the book by Don Freeman

CAST OF CHARACTERS

MOPPY, a young boy.
MOTHER
MR. LAWSON
A WOMAN ON A LADDER
A LADY WITHOUT HER GLASSES
SALESMAN
MR. BARBERPOLI

*(A YOUNG BOY enters dressed in overalls and striped T-shirt and bright, red hair that looks like a mop on his head.)*

**MOPPY:** This is my story. A story of a boy who NEVER wanted to have my hair cut. Everybody calls me Moppy for a reason. Do you think my hair looks like a mop? *(Waits for a response from the children:)* Well, I don't care what anybody says about my hair or what they call me, for that matter. I just want to stay at home and play...do the things that make me happy. I play all sorts of things! Let me show you. *(While he explains, he acts things out for the audience:)* Sometimes I play that I'm a soaring eagle flying over cannons and valleys.

*(The sounds of a FLUTE playing a Native American song.)*

Other times I pretend I'm a roaring lion stalking my prey through the African Savannah.

*(Sounds of AFRICAN TRIBAL MUSIC as he leaps around the stage and growls at the audience.)*

See, I need my hair to look like a lion's mane! You were scared, weren't you?

*(He waits for a response from the audience, very proud of himself. He begins to hang from the branches of a "tree" as his MOTHER enters.)*

**MOTHER:** Pardon me, but who do you think you are dangling there—Tarzan?

**MOPPY:** Oh no, Mother, I'm not Tarzan! I'm a man from Mars and I'm visiting all the stars and other planets!

*(The SOUNDS of MISSION CONTROL during a space mission.)*

**MOTHER:** Well then, Mister Man-from-Mars, could you plan to make a landing on this earth sometime today? We want you to hop on over to hairdresser and get that floppy mop clipped off before your birthday party tomorrow. You want to be able to SEE your presents don't you? You won't if there's a bunch of hair in your eyes. Here's some money. *(Handing it to him. He stuffs it into his pocket:)* I've just called Mr. Barberpoli and he says he'll be ready for you at four o'clock sharp. What time is it now?

*(He looks at his watch.)*

**MOPPY:** It's 3:30 now.

**MOTHER:** Well, let's see you hippity-hop to the barbershop all by yourself.

**MOPPY:** Off I go!

*(He zooms off like a rocket being launched. She laughs and exits. After he rounds the corner though, he loses interest.)*

I don't need my hair cut at all — anyway not now.

*(He walks along until some bright red lollipops catch his eyes in the candy store window. As he is standing there, a SHAGGY DOG, with his eyes hidden, enters and barks at him, wagging his tail. He bends down to pet the pup. The pup rolls on his back for Moppy to scratch his tummy.)*

What a silly-looking pup you are! You're the one who needs a haircut, not me!

*(The shaggy dog barks and exits. Moppy continues to walk until he comes across MR. LAWSON mowing his yard.)*

That lawn is what needs a haircut, not me!

*(Mr. Lawson stops to wipe his brow.)*

**MR. LAWSON:** How about letting me use this machine on that grassy patch of yours, boy? It could do with some mowing.

**MOPPY:** No thanks, Mr. Lawson.

*(He continues on his way. A WOMAN ON A LADDER is snipping branches off a low, droopy tree.)*

**MOPPY:** Maybe a tree needs a clipping, but not me!

**WOMAN ON A LADDER:** Oh, I don't know about that. You could do with a few snips of these snippers, mister!

**MOPPY:** No thanks, ma'am!

*(He skips along until he sees the barbershop. He starts to walk to the door but changes his mind. He turns to address the audience.)*

I just don't want a haircut. I think I'm afraid. Perhaps I'll hide behind this barrel of brooms and brush and fancy mops.

*(He moves behind the barrel. A LADY WITHOUT HER GLASSES approaches the barrel with a SALESMAN.)*

**LADY WITHOUT HER GLASSES:** I'm wanting a mop to help me keep my kitchen floor clean.

**SALESMAN:** We have lots to choose from right over here.

**LADY WITHOUT HER GLASSES:** I want the strongest, fluffiest, floppiest mop you have, sir. Here—this one will do very well. I'll take it along with me right now.

*(She begins shaking the mops, one at a time. Reaching out, she grabs Moppy's hair and pulls it.)*

**MOPPY:** OUCH! Let go! I'm not a mop! I'm a boy!

*(The Lady lets go, and Moppy runs into the barbershop. He rests in the chair in front of the mirror. MR. BARBERPOLI enters.)*

**MR. BARBERPOLI:** I thought maybe you forgot! But you're right on the dot. It's exactly four!

*(He places the cape around Moppy.)*

**MOPPY:** Please, Mr. Barberpoli, don't let me look like a mop anymore. I don't want to clean anybody's kitchen floor!

*(Mr. Barberpoli goes to work. He clips and snips until Moppy looks like a new kid. He holds up a mirror for him to look in when he is finished.)*

**MR. BARBERPOLI:** Well, now, who's that, would you say?

**MOPPY:** It's me! It's me without the floppy old mop on top! Hooray!

*(He hops down and gives Mr. Barberpoli the money and runs out the door.)*

*(To the Audience:)* Look at me! Look at me now! The world looks spick-and-span somehow! Look at the lawn so nicely mowed. And the tree is no longer bowing low.

*(The shaggy pup enters again all trimmed up. Nice and neat.)*

Wow, look at you! You got a haircut too!

*(Mother enters carrying a birthday cake with a number 6 candle.)*

**MOTHER:** I hardly recognize my birthday boy! What does your cake say?

**MOPPY:** "Happy birthday, Marty!" That's my name alright, real and true. And with this haircut I feel brand new.

*(He blows out his candle. Blackout.)*

## The Author Speaks

**Are any characters modeled after real life or historical figures?**
The characters in these plays are taken directly from the books written and illustrated by the late Don Freeman. The books about Corduroy the bear were originally written for his young son, Roy. In fact, the main character was originally his son and not a bear at all. Don Freeman enjoyed capturing the whimsical way life danced around him. He spent time in the theater in his early career and made hundreds of sketches that his son posts from time to time on the website in his father's honor.

**What inspired you to write these plays?**
*A Pocket for Corduroy* was my favorite children's book growing up, and the first book I remember my mother reading over and over to me. I remember the feeling of her warm lap, as we cuddled in a beanbag chair situated in the Children's Corner of the library. She always allowed me to check it out several times. I enjoyed that Lisa, in the story, was an only child, just like me, and believed that her stuffed animals talked to her. Many afternoons you could find me in my room, pretending to have tea parties and adventures with my stuffed animals too. Almost all of Don Freeman's books have animals as the main characters, which offer a fantastic element for productions, regardless if you use actors or puppets.

**Was the structure or other elements of the play influenced by any other work?**
I tried to remain true to the original structure and style of Don Freeman's original work. Adaptation is an art form in itself, as you create the story in a new medium. What might work on the page may not communicate with live actors. I took great

detail in looking at ways to remain true to the themes that Freeman tried to create, with room for creativity as well.

As an educator, I deeply value books that teach children moral lessons. Friendship, Uniqueness, Persistence, Making Mistakes, Being Honest, Believing in yourself, are just some of the many excellent lessons that Don Freeman works explore. My hope was that anyone could produce these pieces as a short piece or a collection to spur on conversations for children and the young at heart.

I received permission to adapt Don Freeman's entire catalogue from his son, Roy Freeman, who currently manages his late father's estate.

**What writers have had the most profound effect on your style?**
For this piece, Don Freeman, of course. I enjoy all types of writers! Interesting word choice, such as David Shannon and fantastic teaching aides for character development, such as Julia Cook. For the play, *Dandelion*, I imagined using an 18-foot giraffe puppet, much like a police bobby that we used in an award-winning production of *A Child's Christmas in Wales* that I performed in. Magically, the world is transformed, as a puppet towers over the other actors, and helps the children see the immensity of a life-size giraffe.

**What do you hope to achieve with this work?**
It is my hope that younger generations will be exposed to and enjoy these delightful stories created by a man who was all heart.

**What were the biggest challenges involved in the writing of this play?**
It was incredibly important to me to get the approval of Don

Freeman's son. The original *Corduroy* books were written about and for him. Because these books are the legacy of a talented man, I wanted to be sure that the themes and characters remained consistent.

**What are the most common mistakes that occur in productions of your work?**
People who don't use their imagination. Look for all the creative possibilities for making the magic come to life. The script is like an empty canvas, the actor becomes the artist.

**What inspired you to become a playwright?**
I have been involved in theater since I was six years old. The magic sunk in. It was a natural process after performing all my life. In the sixth grade, I wrote my first mystery play, which I rehearsed and performed in my back yard. I wanted to write plays that I would enjoy performing in as an actor, directing and leaving as my legacy.

**How did you research the subject?**
I researched the project by speaking with Roy Freeman, and immersing myself in the works of Don Freeman. I tried to get my hands on every book he'd written and/or illustrated. Some were difficult to acquire, as many are no longer in print. Roy Freeman was extremely helpful making sure that I had an accurate list and cheering me on when I got discouraged or stuck. Because Don Freeman is deceased, I had to get to know him through the memories of his son and by letting his work speak to me.

**Do any films/videos exist of prior productions of this play?**
Scholastic has a wonderful animated version of *Corduroy*.

**What other books would you like to adapt?**
I enjoy books that tell a fantastic story with themes that teach us a lesson. One of my favorites is *A Bad Case of Stripes* by David Shannon. It's one of my favorite books to read to my kindergarten students that deals with honesty and individuality. I can't imagine how they would do it on stage, but it would be fabulous to see.

## About the Author

**Wysteria Edwards** is a native of Washington State. She holds her degrees in Education and Theater from Whitworth College (B.A.) and from Washington State University (Ed.M.), a Masters in Reading and Literacy. After participating in the theater for over 25 years, she began the journey of crafting her first script, *Broken Thread*. This script marked her debut as a playwright in Chicago, where she serves as a Resident Playwright/Literary Manager for the Urban Theater Company. Recently she has adapted several works for the stage including ***The Disappeared, Belle Prater's Boy, Dovey Coe***, and the catalogue of Don Freeman picture books. Her play ***Mrs. Murphy's Porch*** was a Play Lab Selection for the Last Frontier Theater Conference (Valdez, AK), and ***The Disappeared*** received an "Honorable Mention" from the She Writes Festival. She is a member of the Dramatists Guild of America, Chicago Dramatists and International Centre for Female Playwrights and the Northwest Playwrights' Alliance. Wysteria has studied privately under the mentorship of Stuart Spencer (NYC) and has participated in workshops with playwrights such as Steven Dietz.

## About YouthPLAYS

**YouthPLAYS** (www.youthplays.com) is a publisher of award-winning professional dramatists and talented new discoveries, each with an original theatrical voice, and all dedicated to expanding the vocabulary of theatre for young actors and audiences. On our website you'll find one-act and full-length plays and musicals for teen and pre-teen (and even college) actors, as well as duets and monologues for competition. Many of our authors' works have been widely produced at high schools and middle schools, youth theatres and other TYA companies, both amateur and professional, as well as at elementary schools, camps, churches and other institutions serving young audiences and/or actors worldwide. Most are intended for performance by young people, while some are intended for adult actors performing for young audiences.

YouthPLAYS was co-founded by professional playwrights Jonathan Dorf and Ed Shockley. It began merely as an additional outlet to market their own works, which included a substantial body of award-winning published and unpublished plays and musicals. Those interested in their published plays were directed to the respective publishers' websites, and unpublished plays were made available in electronic form. But when they saw the desperate need for material for young actors and audiences—coupled with their experience that numerous quality plays for young people weren't finding a home—they made the decision to represent the work of other playwrights as well. Dozens and dozens of authors are now members of the YouthPLAYS family, with scripts available both electronically and in traditional acting editions. We continue to grow as we look for exciting and challenging plays and musicals for young actors and audiences.

## About ProduceaPlay.com

Let's put up a play! Great idea! But producing a play takes time, energy and knowledge. While finding the necessary time and energy is up to you, ProduceaPlay.com is a website designed to assist you with that third element: knowledge.

Created by YouthPLAYS' co-founders, Jonathan Dorf and Ed Shockley, ProduceaPlay.com serves as a resource for producers at all levels as it addresses the many facets of production. As Dorf and Shockley speak from their years of experience (as playwrights, producers, directors and more), they are joined by a group of award-winning theatre professionals and experienced teachers from the world of academic theatre, all making their expertise available for free in the hope of helping this and future generations of producers, whether it's at the school or university level, or in community or professional theatres.

The site is organized into a series of major topics, each of which has its own page that delves into the subject in detail, offering suggestions and links for further information. For example, Publicity covers everything from Publicizing Auditions to How to Use Social Media to Posters to whether it's worth hiring a publicist. Casting details Where to Find the Actors, How to Evaluate a Resume, Callbacks and even Dealing with Problem Actors. You'll find guidance on your Production Timeline, The Theater Space, Picking a Play, Budget, Contracts, Rehearsing the Play, The Program, House Management, Backstage, and many other important subjects.

The site is constantly under construction, so visit often for the latest insights on play producing, and let it help make your play production dreams a reality.

# More from YouthPLAYS

***Queen Zixi of Ix: Or The Story of the Magic Cloak*** by Jason Tremblay
Dramedy. 60-75 minutes. 5-25+ females, 5-25+ males (10-50+ performers possible).

Adapted from the novel by L. Frank Baum, *Queen Zixi of Ix*, critically acclaimed as "one of the best fairy tales ever written by anyone." Bored with their ceaseless dancing, the fairies create a magic cloak which will grant its wearer a single wish. At the same time, the King of Noland has died without an heir, and the law says that the new king shall be the forty-seventh person to enter the city gate that day. And on that day, a humble ferryman's son, Bud, happens to be on his way to the city with his sister, Fluff...

***Sidekickin' It!*** by Adam J. Goldberg
Comedy. 23-30 minutes. 2 females, 6-9 either (8-11 performers possible).

The story of Robin, a precocious girl with gumption beyond her years, and Daybreak, a superhero who finds he will need more than the ability to lift really, really heavy stuff if he is going to stop humanity's destruction at the hands of the diabolical Von Darkness. Watch Robin teach Daybreak that no power is greater than the power of friendship.

***Telling William Tell*** by Evan Guilford-Blake
Dramedy. 80-85 minutes. 7-11 males, 4-10 females (11-21 performers possible).

The children grab the spotlight in this retelling of the story of the mythical Swiss hero—famed for shooting an apple off his son's head—framed by a fictionalized story of Rossini writing his famed opera. Music by the great composer enriches this thrilling tale of Switzerland's fight for freedom and the birth of a new work of musical art.

### *The Story Club* by Nicole B. Adkins
Young Audiences. 45-50 minutes. 1 male, 3 females.

Ivy is used to being the Queen of the Story Club. Everyone agrees she's the best storyteller—that's why *she* gets to make up the stories and cast the parts. But the Queen's subjects are suddenly getting restless: little brother Charlie won't stop practicing karate, her friend Justine starts to get ideas of her own, and then a clever new neighbor arrives just in time to take over Fairy Land!

### *Outside the Box* by Bradley Hayward
Dramedy. 25-35 minutes. 12 either.

Thinking outside the box isn't always easy, especially when the world requires you to live on the inside. Exhausted from cramming into corners where they do not fit, six teenagers turn things inside out by inviting others to see things from a whole new perspective—outside to a world where balloons change color, brooms become dance partners, and kites fly without a string.

### *Dear Chuck* by Jonathan Dorf
Dramedy. 30-40 minutes. 8-30+ performers (gender flexible).

Teenagers are caught in the middle—they're not quite adults, but they're definitely no longer children. Through scenes and monologues, we meet an eclectic group of teens trying to communicate with that wannabe special someone, coping with a classmate's suicide, battling controlling parents, swimming for that island of calm in the stormy sea of technology—and many others. What they all have in common is the search for their "Chuck," that elusive moment of knowing who you are. Also available in a 60-70 minute version.

### *Dodge* by Ed Shockley
Comedy. 25-35 minutes. 6-15 males, 5-15 females (11-30 performers possible).

Dodge disappears after being sent to fetch more gold paint. She's really just trying to avoid the work of painting the leaves for autumn, but the other Elves assume that she has been waylaid by the winter Gnomes—and now war is brewing. Holmstead, a character worthy of Arthur Conan Doyle, sets out with Swallow, following the clues the hapless Dodge has left behind, as Dodge tries desperately to think of a way to return and avert war without revealing her laziness and deception.

### *The Christmas Princess* by Arthur M. Jolly
Fairy Tale. 60-80 minutes (flexible). 4-5+ males, 4-8+ females (8-25 performers possible, including a size and gender-flexible ensemble of dancers).

It's Christmas Eve—and the palace is in turmoil. The next day is not only Christmas, but the wedding day of the beautiful (but spoiled) Princess and the handsome (but dumb as a bag of rocks) Prince Valiant. The problem: the Princess doesn't want to marry a stupid prince. Desperate to find a way out of the marriage, she seeks the advice of Watt the Witch, who sends her on a quest to find three magical gifts that will allow her to escape her wedding.

### *Children of Hooverville* by Hollie Michaels
Drama. 45-55 minutes. 3 males, 10 females (with up to 7 additional non-speaking roles; 13-20 performers possible).

After 13-year-old Elsie Davis loses her family farm to the bank and her brother to the dust storms, she joins family and friends on a forced journey along Route 66 in search of a better life in California. Together they must survive unimaginable hardships and overcome theft, illness and unsympathetic authorities. But when at last they arrive in the Golden State, it may not be the promised land they had hoped for...

Made in the USA
Coppell, TX
14 December 2019